AL LEONARD

TIN WHISTL METHOD

MW00446459

BY SEÁN GAVIN

PLAYBACK+
Speed • Pitch • Balance • Loop

To access audio visit:
www.halleonard.com/mylibrary

Enter Code
1514-2052-6107-9759

ISBN 978-1-5400-2477-0

HAL•LEONARD®

Visit Hal Leonard Online at
www.halleonard.com

Contact us:
Hal Leonard
7777 West Bluemound Road
Milwaukee, WI 53213
Email: info@halleonard.com

In Europe, contact:
Hal Leonard Europe Limited
42 Wigmore Street
Marylebone, London, W1U 2RN
Email: info@halleonardeurope.com

In Australia, contact:
Hal Leonard Australia Pty. Ltd.
4 Lentara Court
Cheltenham, Victoria, 3192 Australia
Email: info@halleonard.com.au

CONTENTS

INTRODUCTION

Welcome to the *Hal Leonard Tin Whistle Method*. This book and the accompanying audio tracks will give you an introduction to the tin whistle and to traditional Irish music. The method outlined in this book is designed for those who are new to playing the tin whistle.

Traditional Irish music is largely an oral tradition and as such, there is no entirely standardized methodology of playing. To paraphrase the legendary flute player, Kevin Henry, "That's what makes our music so intricate. Everyone takes their own interpretation out of it." Indeed, there is a vast array of interpretations among its many exponents throughout Ireland and beyond. There are numerous different styles and approaches. The method outlined in this book is partly inherited from my many great teachers and partly developed from my own years of playing and teaching.

Like any instrument, learning the tin whistle requires dedicated study and practice. The lessons ahead start at a basic level and progress to more advanced tunes and techniques. I recommend students play along with the accompanying audio and try to replicate the notes and sounds discussed in the following pages. Designed for learning, the audio is made up of 25 tunes played at slow, moderate, and faster tempos. There are many great players of the instrument, each with their own different approaches; these are simply mine. Thanks for your interest in Irish music and the tin whistle.

–Seán Gavin

A BRIEF NOTE ON TRADITIONAL IRISH MUSIC AND THE TIN WHISTLE

The tin whistle is also called the Irish whistle, penny whistle, or in the Irish language, *an fheadóg stáin*. Six-holed whistles can be found throughout history in many cultures of the world. Though the origins of traditional Irish music can be dated back hundreds of years, the bulk of the tunes that comprise the tradition were composed during the 17th, 18th, and 19th centuries. Some tunes are older while others are being written today, but they all are part of a common repertoire enjoyed by Irish musicians everywhere. The tin whistle is one of the quintessential instruments of the tradition and has been immortalized in the recordings of such greats as Micho Russell, Paddy Breen, Jim Donoghue, Kevin Henry, and Mary Bergin, among many more.

PARTS OF THE TIN WHISTLE

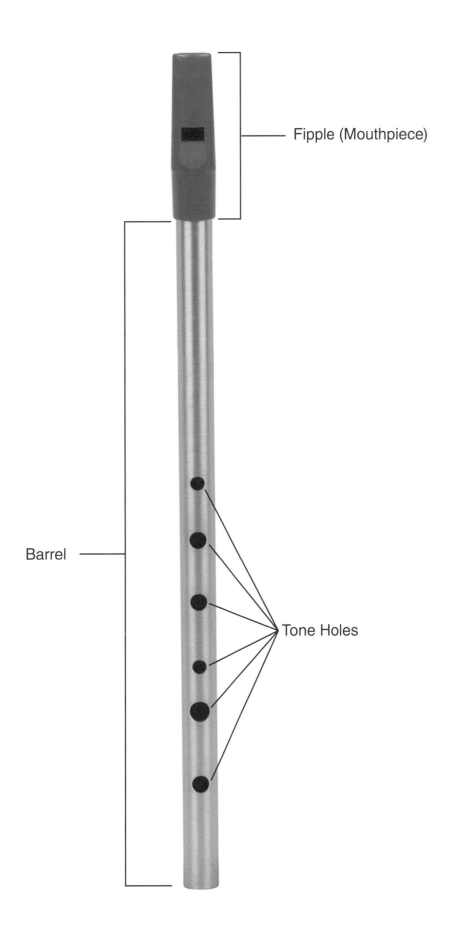

Fipple (Mouthpiece)

Barrel

Tone Holes

*Some whistles also have an adjustable slide, separating the top and bottom parts to allow for tuning.

STARTING TO PLAY THE TIN WHISTLE

BLOWING THE WHISTLE

Blow into the mouthpiece of the whistle to generate a sound. If your fingers are not covering any of the tone holes, the note you're playing is C#. If you blow with a moderate amount of pressure, you should be able to keep the pitch steady for at least ten seconds. Be careful: Blowing too hard will cause the octave to jump up, and blowing too soft will cause the pitch and tone to be inconsistent.

When first playing this note, it may feel like the instrument isn't balanced. Don't worry, that will improve with practice. To help with this problem, place both thumbs on the back of the whistle to help stabilize the instrument. You can also use your pinky on the bottom hand to help stabilize the whistle, but it is not essential.

Keep in mind to always breathe from your mouth, never your nose. Your breath should generate from your diaphragm, so your belly should expand when you breathe, not your chest.

COVERING THE HOLES

For right-handed whistlers, cover the top three tone-holes of the whistle using your index finger, middle finger, and ring finger on your left hand. It should be emphasized that the *left hand goes on top*. Then, using the same fingers on your right hand, cover the remaining three tone-holes. Left-handed players can choose to play with the left or right hand on top. The book is written under the assumption that your left hand will be on top.

If your fingers are completely sealing the tone holes, preventing any air from escaping, you should now be able to play the note low D. If you're unable to play the note clearly, there may be air escaping from one or more of the tone holes. If this is happening, the note will not fully sound. Make sure that your fingers are completely covering the holes to prevent this and further issues with your tone and pitch.

READING NOTES AND SCALES

Once you're able to play the low D consistently, it's time to learn notes and scales. Before you learn the first scale, please review the following terms and definitions.

Staff: These five lines, with four spaces in between, is known as a *staff*. When reading music, all of the notes will appear on, above, or below the staff.

Treble Clef: This symbol determines which notes will be signified by the lines and spaces of the staff. There are other clefs, but treble clef is the one we'll use for the whistle.

Sharp: A *sharp* is indicated by the symbol, ♯ A sharp raises the pitch of a natural note (one of the white keys on the piano) by a half-step. A note without the symbol is natural, but it can also be indicated with this symbol: ♮. For our purposes, sharps are mostly used to indicate key signatures. (We will not see the use of the natural symbol throughout the book, either.)

Key Signature: The *key signature* appears on the staff just after the treble clef. It lets you know what key a tune is in and which notes to play sharp. For this book, we only need to know two key signatures.

D major, which has two sharps:

G major, which has one sharp:

Now let's learn the corresponding scales.

THE D MAJOR SCALE

Using the fingering chart below, practice playing up and down the D major scale.

- Memorize the name of each note and where it falls on the staff.

- The key signature has two sharps, F♯ and C♯. All F's and C's must be played sharp when playing in this key.

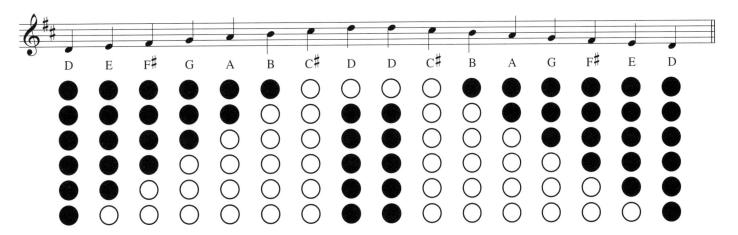

Note: The fingering for the high D is different than the low D.

THE G MAJOR SCALE

Using the fingering chart below, practice playing up and down the G major scale.

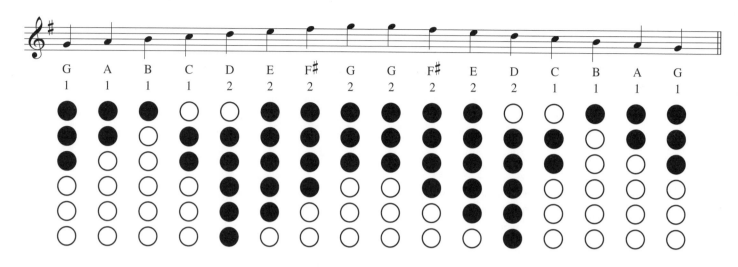

- This scale crosses from the whistle's first octave to its second. (The octaves are denoted above the fingerings.)

- Achieve the second octave by blowing harder.

- The key signature has only one sharp, F#.

- When the key signature does not list C#, you play C natural. Note that the fingering for C natural is different.

Using just these two scales, you can learn to play tunes in many different keys. (We will touch more on this later.)

Here are some visual representations of the notes above.

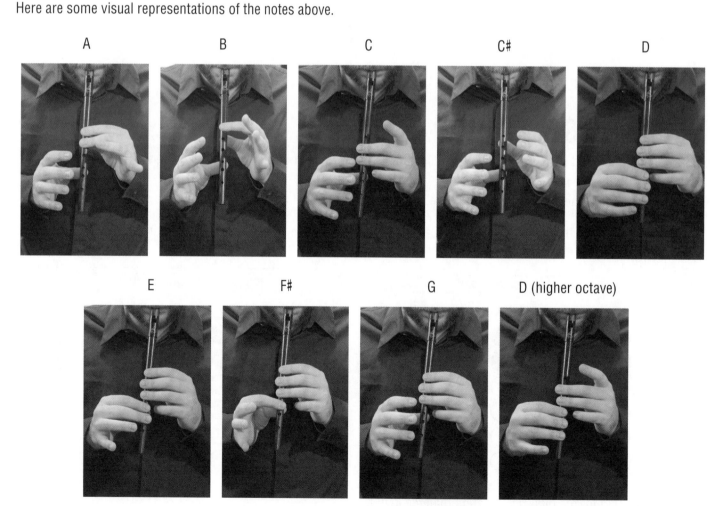

READING RHYTHMS

Now that you have learned how to play the G major and D major scales and how to read the notes on the staff, it's time to learn how to read the rhythmic part of music notation.

Measures and Bar Lines: Using bar lines, the staff is divided into units called *measures*, each of which contains a certain number of beats. A *double bar line* marks the end of a part or section.

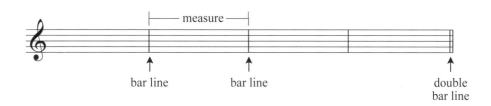

Note Duration: A written note has a relative duration in time as well as a pitch. We'll use *quarter* notes, *eighth* notes (twice as fast as quarter notes), and *16th* notes (twice as fast as eighth notes).

Quarter Note ♩	= 2 eighth notes	Not Beamed in Groups ♩♩
Eighth Note ♪	= 1/2 a quarter note	Beamed in Groups ♫
16th Note ♬	= 1/2 an eighth note	Beamed in Groups ♬

Time Signature: The time signature, written as two numbers after the treble clef, describes the rhythmic pattern of the music. The bottom number indicates what kind of note will be the rhythmic unit for each measure. The top number is how many of those units will be in each measure. Below are some common time signatures.

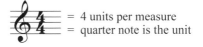 = 4 units per measure
= quarter note is the unit

= 2 units per measure
= quarter note is the unit

= 6 units per measure
= eighth note is the unit

COUNTING IN 4/4

Count to four at a steady pace. The numbers represent quarter notes. Then, say "and" between the numbers. Now each number, as well as each "and," represents an eighth note. Each number is a *downbeat*, while each "and" is an *upbeat*. Count while clapping out or playing the following. Tap your foot on the downbeats.

To count out 16th notes, add "e" after each number and "a" after each "and."

You can also associate some rhythmic units with words. For an eighth note followed by two 16ths, like in the second measure, say "grasshopper." For two 16ths followed by an eighth, say "butterfly."

DOTTED NOTES

A dot after a note adds half of the note's value.

Dotted Quarter Note

Dotted Eighth Note

Don't worry if you find it tricky to count out dotted eighths for now. It will be much easier with the recordings later.

PUTTING THE PIECES TOGETHER

MARY HAD A LITTLE LAMB

Use this familiar nursery rhyme to practice the skills you've learned so far. It's in 2/4 time, not 4/4, so there are only two quarter notes per measure. Otherwise, it's counted out the same way.

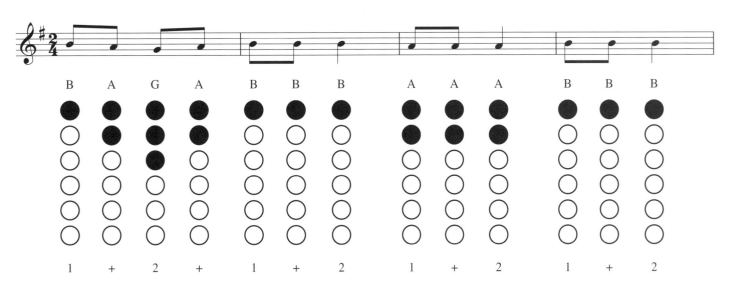

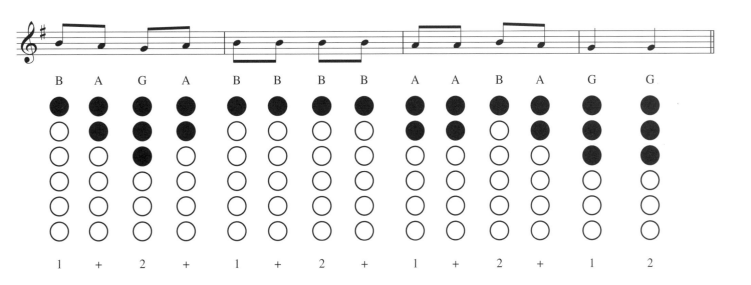

Note: If you have already played a wind instrument in a classical or school band setting, you may be inclined to articulate each note with tonguing. But this will not be suitable when we get into Irish music. For now, don't assume any default articulation. (If not, then you needn't worry about this.)

Listening and Memorizing

For Irish music, you must listen and memorize the melodies. Practice memorization on "Mary Had a Little Lamb," even if you can easily read it. Break it down into sections.

Step 1: Memorize the first two measures. This is the first phrase of the tune.

Step 2: Move on to the second phrase, also two measures.

Step 3: Combine the first and second phrases. Repeat until it comes naturally.

Step 4: The third phrase begins just like the first. Memorize the part that's different.

Step 5: Learn the fourth and final phrase, completing the tune.

Step 6: Combine the third and fourth phrases. This is the second half of the tune. Repeat it until it comes naturally.

Step 7: Play the entire melody without looking at the music. Keep repeating it until it becomes very natural and won't be forgotten.

This is how you must approach each tune in this book. Start with at most one line of a tune, and play it many times until it becomes natural and you can play it without reading it. When a measure gives you trouble, repeat that measure by itself several times.

Breathing

Where and how to breathe is very important. Imagine singing the lyrics:

"Mary had a little lamb, little lamb, little lamb."

It's natural to pause after the word "*lamb*" each time. That corresponds with the quarter notes in the melody. Do the same when playing it on the whistle. Shorten the quarter notes enough to take a breath at the end of each one. You can play just the first half of the note and breathe during the second half. Typically, you must skip at least the space of an eighth note to allow for your breath.

Now try to play the same melody in a different key, D major. (The grey notes are suggested for breathing.)

Now try to play the same melody one octave higher. To reach the second octave, blow harder.

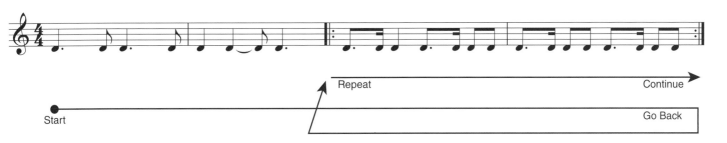

Repeats and Parts

Often a section of music is to be repeated. Rather than write it out again, a *repeat* symbol at the end of a measure means to go back to the beginning and repeat what you have played so far once more before going on.

The same symbol facing the other way at the beginning of a measure means to go back and repeat from that measure.

Tune Structure

Irish tunes are usually divided into parts that are repeated before continuing. There will usually be an A part and a B part. After playing each part twice, it's understood to return to the beginning and do it again. The pattern is AA BB AA BB and so on. The entire tune is repeated a few times before switching to another tune. The number of repeats varies with the players. When learning a new tune, you should repeat it many times.

POLKAS

An *Irish polka* is a quick, 2/4 dance tune associated more with the southwest, especially County Kerry. It isn't very similar to its famous eastern European cousin. The polka is often a first tune for Irish music learners. Recall that a dotted eighth note is equal to three 16th notes.

A dotted eighth note followed by a 16th note takes the same time as two eighth notes, but the first note is longer and the second one is shorter.

BRITCHES FULL OF STITCHES

If you find it difficult to count out this rhythm, just listen to the audio track. It's much easier to listen and repeat than to count it out. Besides, there are other aspects of rhythm and phrasing you can only learn by listening. Try to imitate the variations in note length and emphasis that you hear on the recording. The grey notes are suggested for breathing, and the notes above which a dagger (†) appears denote instances of variation. Remember that for Irish music, you need to listen and memorize the tune, rather than relying on the sheet music. Repeat the entire tune many times.

THE KERRY POLKA

With this tune we introduce *ornamentation*. Irish musicians employ various ornaments. The first one to learn is the *grace note*. It can be used as a rhythmic embellishment, to decorate the melody, or to distinguish repeated notes, as we will do here. In general, you should place grace notes on stressed notes. In the notation, the grace note appears before the second E, but it's more accurate to think of it as occurring directly on the second E.

Grace Note on E

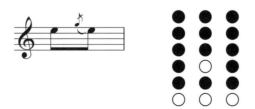

Play the E, then quickly lift and return the index finger on your right hand. Something like a G note will sound very quickly, separating what essentially sounds like two Es. Listen to the slow version of the tune on the audio track for an example.

To advance further, try picking up some of the extra notes from the fast version. A great Donegal fiddler named Neilidh Boyle once said, "The sheet music is simply the bones. You must put the beef on it!"

O'CONNOR'S POLKA 🔊

For this tune, we will introduce another grace note, this time on a B.

Grace Note on B

Perform the grace note by simply lifting your left index finger. The grace note will actually be a C♯, which is not in the key signature, but that will not be noticeable. To avoid cluttering the music, it will be notated as a regular C. Listen to the audio track to hear the placement of each grace note.

Remember that the grey notes are suggested for breathing. You don't have to breathe on every one of them. Vary your choices as you repeat the tune many times. You can shorten the grey quarter notes to take a breath, or skip the grey eighth notes entirely. Try to imitate the variations in note length, emphasis, and breathing from the recording. Listen to the melody and memorize it by breaking it down, rather than relying only on the sheet music.

KNOCKNAGASHEL POLKA

I learned this polka from the well-known accordion player and singer from West Kerry, Séamus Begley. It's a simple tune, but it's very effective if played well. Continue to work on breathing, phrasing, listening, and memorizing.

For further advancement, try to learn the extra bits on the audio track. You can also return to it and any other tune after you've become more advanced.

JIGS

Jigs are widely associated with Irish music. They are in 6/8 time, meaning there are six eighth notes per measure.

To count out note values in 6/8, count to six. Each number is an eighth note. Quarter notes last for two counts while dotted quarter notes last for three.

But don't think of the eighth note values as six independent beats. It's better to think of two larger beats, each of which is divided into three eighth notes. Tap your foot twice per measure, on beats 1 and 4. (These are the downbeats.)

SWING

Swing refers to an unwritten rhythm. Irish jigs have their own kind of swing. The first six notes above are all eighth notes, but they should not be given exactly equal length. The first note in a group is often played longer, and the second note shorter, than their written values. Stress, or emphasis, is another aspect of swing that isn't notated. Swing is too irregular to be written out effectively. You must listen carefully and repeat what you hear.

One useful trick is to think of the word "emphasis, emphasis…" being repeated, or the phrase "rashers and sausages…"

TÁ AN COILEACH AG FÓGAIRT AN LAE

This tune, which roughly translates to "When the Cock Crows It Is Day," is a great first jig to learn. Like many jigs, it is the melody of a song with words, as opposed to something solely instrumental in nature. Listening to the song associated with a tune, or better still, learning to sing the words, will help you to render its lyrical quality.

Remember: Listen to the audio track to get a feel for the swing. Break it down and memorize it. Pay attention to your breathing and grace notes.

"Tá An Coileach Ag Fógairt An Lae" appears on the next page to allow for easier reading.

First Verse:

Tá 'n coileach ag fógairt an lae.

Tá 'n coileach ag fógairt an lae.

Tá an mhuc ag an doras

ag iarraidh é a oscailt.

Tá 'n coileach ag fógairt an lae.

Translation:

When the cock crows, it is day.

When the cock crows, it is day.

The pig is at the door,

Wanting it opened.

The cock is announcing the day.

ORNAMENTATION: ROLLS

It's time to learn the quintessential Irish ornament: the *roll*. A roll usually takes the place of a dotted quarter note, or three eighth notes. We use the *turn* symbol to indicate a roll.

It is often described as containing five notes, but it might be easier to think of it as three eighth notes, separated by two grace notes. First is a regular grace note, and then a tap, or a grace note from below. To execute a tap, briefly touch the hole beneath the note you're playing.

Try a roll on an F# When starting out, it's easier to play the three eighth notes equally. Later, you can play them in jig rhythm. Play the first F# normally. Grace the second F# from above, as discussed previously, by lifting and returning the left ring finger. Grace the final F# from below, by tapping with the right middle finger. The entire roll is continuously blown. Listen to the audio track to hear an F# roll in the context of a tune. The sheet music shows where it occurs.

Practice your F# roll by trying it many times with a note separating each attempt. Repeat this line.

THE HUMOURS OF GLENDART 🔊

Practice your F# rolls by incorporating them into this classic jig. Listen to the audio track a few times to become familiar with the melody and for an example of an F# roll. Then, try to play slowly through the notation. First, learn the melody with the phrasing. After you've memorized the melody, try including the rolls and grace notes.

* 2nd time only.

THE LILTING BANSHEE

Another common session tune, this jig is ideal for practicing grace notes. Let's also introduce another roll—the low G roll.

Roll on G

Use the ring finger of your left hand for the first grace note and the index finger of your right hand for the second one.

Listen to the audio track a few times to get the melody into your head. Then, try playing through the notation slowly. Practice the grace notes and rolls, and remember to pay attention to phrasing, rhythm, and breathing.

* 2nd time only.

ARTICULATIONS: STACCATO

Staccato means "detached" in Italian. It is the classical term for a note that is articulated to create separation from other notes. The general idea is to have a very brief silence on both sides of the note. The symbol to play a note staccato is a small dot above or below the note.

Here are two ways you can create staccato notes.

- **Tonguing:** To tongue a note, block the passage of air through your mouth using your tongue. Examples are the words, "Ta, ta, ta; da, da, da; ka, ka, ka." Try making the same sounds while blowing the whistle. You can use the passage above to practice it.

- **Glottal stopping:** Say the phrase, "Uh oh." At the end of each word is a glottal stop. You use your throat (your epiglottis) to stop your air before it gets to your mouth. Do the same thing while playing the whistle to quickly blow notes individually.

Tonguing blocks the air from leaving your mouth. Glottal stopping blocks your air from entering your mouth. I use both methods when playing the whistle.

PRACTICING STACCATO

Try rapidly playing many notes while keeping them separate from each other using glottal stopping, tonguing, or a combination of the two.

Placement

Staccato notes are played shorter than others, so place them on short notes in the swing. In a jig, it is common to make the second note in a group of three eighth notes staccato, especially in the case of repeated notes. But if a repeated note falls on a downbeat, it's usually better to distinguish it with a grace note instead. Staccato notes aren't usually notated in Irish music. Some suggestions will be made later, but for now, just experiment. Avoid using them in the same places all the time or creating a consistent repetitive pattern with them.

JIM WARD'S JIG 🔊

Jim Ward was a flute and banjo player from County Clare and played with the famous Kilfenora Ceili Band. He composed this jig which has become a common tune in Irish music. In it, we include both a grace note and a roll on A.

Grace Note on A

Roll on A

Before trying to play the tune, listen to the audio track a few times to become familiar with it. As you learn it, try imitating some of the staccato notes. Aim for about one staccato note per measure.

* 2nd time only.

22

NOTES ABOVE THE STAFF

Some notes go above the staff. An additional line called a *ledger line* is drawn through or underneath them, extending the staff pattern upwards. The following notes are all in the whistle's second octave, so blow harder to reach them.

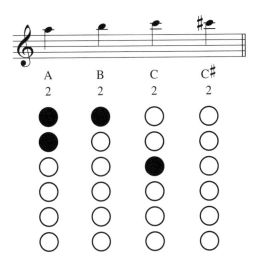

The high C and C# are used almost exclusively as ornaments. It is not necessary to distinguish between them in this context. You simply raise your left index finger. If you are gracing an A, the grace note will be a C. If gracing a B, then a C#. The distinction is not important and will not be notated. You need only memorize the first three notes above the staff.

PLAYING THE HIGH NOTES

Play through this line once or twice just to get used to reading notes above the staff.

MINOR KEYS: THE DORIAN SCALE

The notes of the major scale can also be used to play in minor keys. Compared to major keys, minor keys sound darker, more foreboding. Irish music tends to use a special kind of minor key called *Dorian*.

A MINOR (DORIAN) SCALE

The A minor (Dorian) scale uses the same notes as the G major scale, but it starts and ends on A. When a tune is based around A, but uses these notes, it's in the key of A minor (Dorian). If you have learned the standard minor scale elsewhere, you may notice the difference is that the sixth step in the scale is one half step higher in the Dorian. If not, then you needn't worry about it.

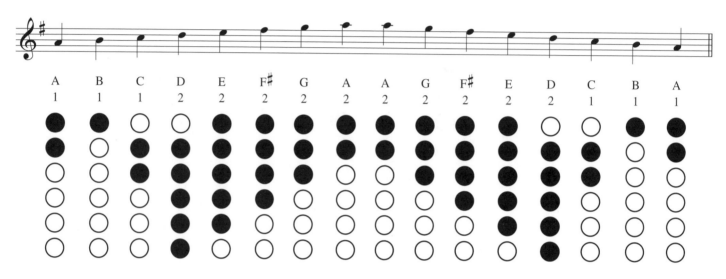

E MINOR (DORIAN) SCALE

Just as the A minor (Dorian) scale uses the same notes as the G major scale, the E minor (Dorian) scale uses those of the D major scale, but it starts and ends on E. When a tune is based around E, but uses these notes, it's in the key of E minor (Dorian).

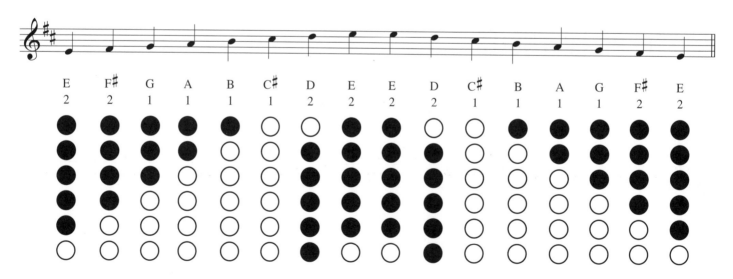

GALLAGHER'S FROLICS 🔊

This is one I learned from Detroit-area piper, Terrence McKinney. It's our first tune in the key of E minor (Dorian), and the first to use nearly the full range of the instrument. It also includes two new rolls on E and B. Try them before learning the tune. Then, listen to the audio track and start breaking it down.

E Roll

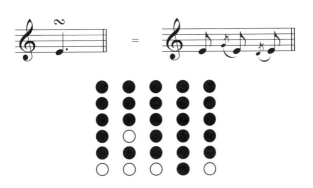

B Roll

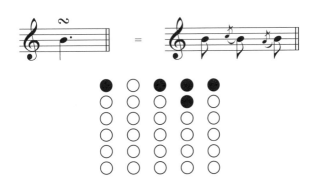

* 2nd time only.

REVIEW OF KEY CONCEPTS

Breathing and Phrasing:

- A grey note is recommended for breathing. You don't have to breathe on every one of them, just some. If it's an eighth note, skip it. If it's a quarter note, cut it in half, breathing on the second half.

- These are not the only good places to breathe; they're just recommendations. Try experimenting with breathing in other places throughout the tune.

- Remember, any time you take a breath, you must skip the space of an eighth note!

Rhythm and Phrasing:

- Don't just play straight eighth notes as written. In a jig, the first note of three eighth notes is often elongated and the second note shortened.

- Varying note length and emphasis creates interesting groupings.

Ornamentation:

- Rolls take up the space of a dotted quarter note or three eight notes.

- The rolls written in the notation are suggestions. There may be other places to play rolls. Experiment!

- Grace notes should be placed only on downbeats in jigs.

Articulation:

- Don't forget to make some notes staccato using glottal stopping and/or tonguing.

- Only play staccato on the short notes in the swing. In a jig, that's usually the second in a group of three eighth notes.

- Try playing at least one staccato note per measure.

Listening:

- For Irish music, listening is more important than reading the notation. You should be able to sing the tune or hear it in your head before you attempt to play it.

- Listen for the extra bits that aren't notated: swing, phrasing, ornaments, extra notes, variations, and articulations.

Try out what you've learned on the following tunes!

SADDLE THE PONY

This is a common session tune many players learn as one of their first jigs. It is a simple tune with a lot of repetition, but it also leaves plenty of space for interpretation and ornamentation.

Before beginning the tune, practice the high G roll.

High G Roll

Use the left ring finger to grace the G from above. Then, use your right index finger to grace from below.

Listen to the audio track to get a feel for the tune before giving it a try.

AN RÓGAIRE DUBH

"An Rógaire Dubh," or in English, "The Black Rogue," is the melody of a song from Connemara, County Galway. It tells the story of a mischievous crow who steals a handkerchief out of a man's pocket.

First Verse:

Tá mo stoca is mo bhróga ag an rógaire dubh,

Tá mo stoca is mo bhróga ag an rógaire dubh,

Tá mo stoca is mo bhróga ag an rógaire dubh,

Mo naipicín póca le bliain is an lá inniu.

Translation:

The black rogue has my socks and my shoes,

The black rogue has my socks and my shoes,

The black rogue has my socks and my shoes,

And my pocket handkerchief a year and a day today.

D Grace Note

Play a D grace note by lifting the third finger of your left hand. You can also experiment with using other fingers.

Listen to the audio track before playing the tune. Some recommendations for staccato are included.

* 2nd time only.

YOUNG TOM ENNIS 🔊

Tom Ennis was an early 20th-century uillean piper from Chicago, the youngest member of the Chicago Irish music club. His record company (Gaelic Records) made some of the earliest commercial recordings of Irish music. Listen to the audio track a few times to become familiar with this jig.

PHRASING

Irish music must be played in phrases rather than as a series of straight, undifferentiated eighth notes. *Phrases* are groups of notes that function in relation to each other to create conflict and resolution in the melody. Mark the boundaries of phrases with breaths.

Think of the first phrase ending on G in the last measure (see arrow) and the following notes as the pickup notes for the next phrase.

The second phrase ends with A (see arrow) while the following B becomes a pickup note for the next phrase.

Remember that grey notes can be replaced by breaths, and playing those notes will elongate the phrase, combining it with the following phrase.

The last phrase of the first part is the concluding phrase, which resolves the tension created by the part so far.

The first phrase in the second part also ends on G, just like the in the first part. Think of this like a rhyme scheme in poetry. The F# becomes a pickup note.

The second phrase of the second part ends on high A, but playing the B makes a nice change. Experiment with both.

Just like in the first part, the third phrase is the same as the first. This is very common throughout Irish music.

The concluding phrase of the second part is the same as the first ending of the first part, which is also common.

THE FROST IS ALL OVER 🔊

This jig is another song melody, this time in English. This setting of the "Frost Is All Over" was recorded by uilleann piper, singer, and folklorist Séamus Ennis. We include a grace note that doesn't come between repeated notes, which is trickier to execute.

Grace Note from a Different Note

While playing the E, lift your left ring finger and your right middle finger simultaneously. Don't raise your right index finger! Then, very quickly return only the left ring finger. Practice the grace note on the passage above before learning the tune. Listen to the audio track a few times and then try playing along.

Lilting

The first part of the song "The Frost Is All Over" has lyrics and the second part is lilted. *Lilting* is a form of *port an bhéil*, or "mouth music," using nonsense vocables to sing a melody. Lilting and singing are good ways to practice creating phrases, especially for whistle players, because of the need to breathe when singing. Séamus Ennis' recording of this tune can be found online. Listen to it for a good example of lilting, and then try singing the song.

What would you do if the ket-tle boiled o - ver? What would I do? On - ly fill it a - gain. And

what would you do if the cow ate the clo - ver? What would I do on - ly set it a - gain.

Dee dai - del dee did - dle dee - yai - del dee - yum, dee - yoo - dle dee dai - del dee - yah! Ti - yoo - dle dum

dee - dle da - lah da li - dee da - lah. Dee yoo ta - tum dah, dee yoo - dle um num.

HORNPIPES

Hornpipes are in 4/4 time. They are usually played with swing, like jigs, but with an extra note at the end. Hornpipes tend to have longer phrases that repeat less often, except that the end of the tune is often the end from the first part. Despite the time signature, most people tap their foot twice per measure, on the first and third counts. But you can still count the rhythms out in 4/4 if you find it helpful. Try tapping your foot along to the audio track for "The Boys of Bluehill."

Tap   Tap   Tap   Tap   Tap   Tap   Tap   Tap

Hornpipe phrases often last about two measures, or four taps. Think about where phrases begin and end as you learn new tunes. Hornpipes also commonly include triplets, three notes played over the space of two eighth notes. The three notes are beamed together and there is a small "3" written underneath.

You can get the triplet rhythm easily using syllables or lilting. The nonsense word, "diddly," with three syllables, like "did-il-ee," falls naturally into the right pattern. Sing along with the same audio track.

Doo - tle   dum   a   doh   lam - a   dee   the   did - il - ee   oh!   Dal - the...

THE BOYS OF BLUEHILL

This is a popular hornpipe that many players learn as one of their first. Listen to the audio track for the rhythms discussed above, and then start breaking it down.

NEW ORNAMENTS AND ACCIDENTALS

On our next tune, "Cronin's Hornpipe," we incorporate consecutive grace notes and accidentals. Try them out before proceeding to the tune.

CONSECUTIVE GRACE NOTES

This is a common ornament in Irish music. The rhythm is slightly different than consecutive triplets. Compare the two.

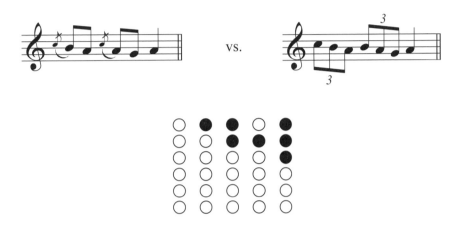

For the figure on the left, you start with no fingers down, and quickly bring down the left index, followed by the middle. Then, grace with the index again. It's rhythmically closer to four notes than to six. Remember, it doesn't matter that the grace note is technically a C#

Trills

Another common ornamentation is a *trill*. It's played similarly to the other ornamentations you've encountered so far, but you begin the trill with the target note, lift your finger, and then return it to its original placement.

ACCIDENTALS

An *accidental* is a note which does not normally appear in the given key. "Cronin's" is in the key of G, which normally uses C natural. But there is a C# near the beginning of the second part—an accidental. An accidental must be specially notated with the # symbol in front of the note.

CRONIN'S HORNPIPE 🔊

Padraig O'Keefe, Dennis Murphy, and Julia Clifford were fiddlers from the Sliabh Luacra region in southwestern Ireland famous for this tune and many more. Look them up for instructive listening.

Listen to the audio track until you have the melody in your head before starting to work your way through "Cronin's Hornpipe." Use what you've learned about consecutive grace notes, trills, and accidentals.

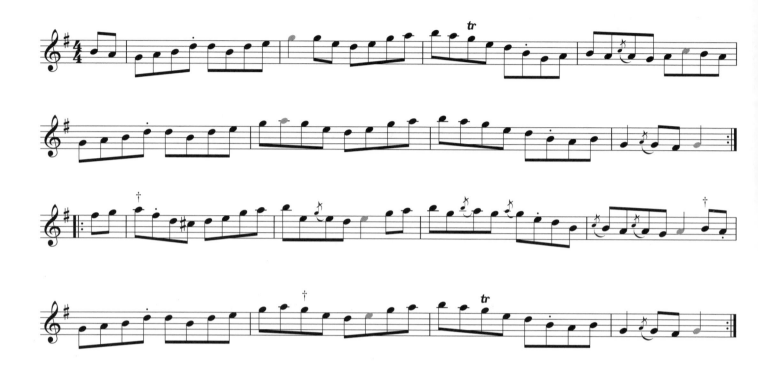

OFF TO CALIFORNIA 🔊

This tune is yet another collected by Captain Francis O'Neill. It's a very common session tune that contains grace notes and rolls. Listen to the audio track a few times before giving it a try.

Phrasing Notes

Use the quarter note to mark the end of this first phrase.

Treat the last two notes of the previous measure as pickup notes for the next phrase.

Treat the third phrase essentially the same as the first.

Make the end of the first part sound conclusive. Breathing on the last quarter note is optional.

At the end of the first phrase of the second part, skip the D and breathe to make the B feel like a quarter note.

Note: The next three phrases of the second part are the same as the corresponding phrases from the first part. (This is common in hornpipes.) But vary the ornamentation and/or breathing a bit.

Turn to the next page to play "The Humours of Tullycrine."

THE HUMOURS OF TULLYCRINE 🔊

This hornpipe was collected from County Clare fiddler John Kelly. Tullycrine is a townland near Kilrush in southwest County Clare. Before you learn it, listen to the audio track to become familiar with it.

Variation

Let's use this tune to experiment with variation. Variation in Irish music does not normally abandon the melody completely like free improvisation. But you don't play it the same way every time. Here are some ideas for variations on the first phrase. After you can play the basic melody, try them out. Then, use similar ideas to vary other phrases.

HALF NOTES AND CUT TIME

Before the next tune, we introduce some new concepts. So far, we have used quarter notes, eighth notes, and 16th notes. A *half* note is twice as long as a quarter note.

In 4/4, a half note gets two counts. Try tapping while humming or playing the rhythms below.

Now we introduce a new time signature, 2/2, which is closely related to 4/4.

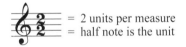

When counting out rhythms in 2/2, you count to 2, like in 2/4. But all the note values are cut in half.

Since the notes have half their usual values, 2/2 is also known as *cut time*. The time signature can be written as 2/2 or with the symbol ¢. Theoretically, measures in 2/2 notate the very same rhythms they do in 4/4, but with different numbers. You can even count them out that way if you need to.

But you will tend to play the rhythms slightly differently if you count two beats instead of four. The pulse of the music naturally divides into groups of two beats rather than four. Cut time music also tends to be played faster than music in 4/4.

REELS

Reels are somewhat like hornpipes. But they are faster, the swing is a little different, the phrases are generally shorter and more repetitive, and they are in cut time. The rhythm is eighth notes in groups of four, the first of which is a downbeat, which is where you tap your foot. Listen to the audio track "O'Connell's Trip to Parliament" for an example. Tap your foot twice per measure.

When you play reels, the notes on those taps should be slightly accented.

STACCATO REVISITED

Recall that staccato notes are separated from surrounding notes by an articulation, either tonguing or glottal stopping. They are notated with a dot above or below the note.

Hopefully you've been experimenting with them a bit. From here on, specific suggestions will be made more frequently. The general idea is to place them on short notes in the swing. In a reel, this occurs on beats 2 and 4 in a group of four eighth notes.

O'CONNELL'S TRIP TO PARLIAMENT 🔊

This reel is named after Daniel O'Connell, known as the "Great Liberator" in Irish history. It's an old uilleann piping tune that also sits quite nicely on the whistle. In this tune, you'll play staccato notes, BCD triplets, and F# rolls. Listen to the audio track and play along as best you can. The C# staccato notes are particularly important in this tune. They always fall on the second part in a group of four eighth notes.

MOTHER AND CHILD 🔊

This tune is often associated with the legendary West Clare flute and whistle player, Micho Russell. Micho often had words for his tunes, and this one is no exception. There is a variation on the ending that makes for a nice transition into the repeat of the tune. The phrases are particularly well defined in this tune, another trademark of the playing of Micho Russell. Notice how the phrases all end with longer notes and that the phrases aren't combined to be played continually as often as in other tunes. Listen to the audio track to hear the tune. Try playing the alternate ending on the second time through the tune.

THE PRIMROSE LASS 🔊

This is a great reel that is also played as a *schottische*. It's often played before "Green Grow the Rushes O." Both were recorded by Sligo flute player Eddie Cahill as well as the renowned Irish band De Dannan.

This tune is full of great places to breathe. Remember that skipping any second or fourth eighth note is worth trying, even if it doesn't end up working. Below are some of the breaths I think help keep the tune fresh and prevent the rhythm from becoming monotonous. Those same notes are also the ones to try making staccato. Again, some may work better than others. Keep the ones you like and don't bother with the others. Listen to the audio track a few times before trying to play along.

BILLY BROCKER

This simple reel is one I associate with the playing of the McDonagh brothers of Ballinafad. I've written the repeats for the parts in the notation to help give a sense of variation in the phrasing, the ornamentation, and the melody. None of these are set in stone; they're merely suggestions. Experiment with changing the breaths, staccato notes, and ornaments. Listen to the audio track to hear how this one sounds.

Variation: Compare the second measure of the first and second lines.

First Time Around

Play an F# roll and breathe in between the G's.

Second Time Around

Replace the F# roll with grace notes followed by D, and then play a roll on G.

Try something similar on other tunes as well!

THE CLOGHER REEL

I associate this reel with Kevin Henry, the great Sligo flute and whistle player. It was one of Kevin's signature tunes, which he recorded on the album *One's Own Place*. There's something special about Kevin's phrasing which really brings out the poetry in the tune like no one else. I've tried to transcribe some of his breathing using the grey notes. It's also a good reel to practice your A rolls. Listen to the audio track until you're ready to play through it.

There are some options for ending this tune and others like it.

Bump Ending

Finish with the D. (Cut the note off relatively quickly.)

Drag Ending

Continue through and end on the first note of the first part. You can also hold the E for a while.

Resolve Ending

Wind down to an A. (This one takes a bit of variation.)

THE FERMOY LASSES 🔊

This reel is a great one for practicing E rolls. Micho Russel also had a great version of this with some unique phrasing and ornamentation. The first part of the tune is in E minor (not Dorian) and the second part is in G major.

THE SLIGO MAID 🔊

One of the most classic reels, "The Sligo Maid" is one of many tunes I learned from my father, Mick Gavin. This tune has a variation on the beginning of the second part, but that variation is only played on the repeat of the part. Practice the variation when playing the tune. Listen to the audio track for reference.

* 2nd time only.

Variation: B Section, Measure 1

You can place a variation like this one in many other tunes as well. Basically, you begin with the note that normally concludes a phrase—A in this case—before returning to it on the next beat in a way that resembles the lead-up to the next phrase. The rhythmic pattern gets doubled, and it's like having two big cheers, one after another!

ABBEY REEL

This tune first appeared in Breandán Breathnach's *Tacar Port* under the name "Ríl Roideacáin" or "Redican's Reel." The source for the tune was accordion player Sonny Brogan. I originally learned it from Dublin flute player Paul McGrattan. Like "The Clogher Reel," this tune ends on the first note of the first part, rather than the last note of the second part. (See below for more info.) Listen to the audio track to hear the whole tune and the ending.

Resolve Ending

End this tune on the very first note instead of the last note. This will provide a better sense of resolution.

STRINGING TUNES TOGETHER

The practice in Irish music is to play one tune a few times before switching to another—in other words, to create *medleys*. Here are some suggestions for creating medleys, using the tunes you have learned in this book.

1. "Jim Ward's"/"Tá An Coileach Ag Fógairt An Lae"

2. "Saddle the Pony"/"Gallagher's Frolics"/"The Frost Is All Over"

3. "Humours of Tullycrine"/"Cronin's Hornpipe"

4. "Abbey Reel"/"Primrose Lass"

5. "Billy Brocker"/"O'Connell's Trip to Parliament"

Try creating medleys of your own with the tunes you've learned so far, and with those you learn going forward. You should usually medley tunes of the same type, although some advanced players will switch from a jig to a reel or from a hornpipe to a reel. Decide if you like the change of key from one tune to another, or phrases in the two that complement each other. Have fun!

INDEX OF CONCEPTS AND TERMS

ACKNOWLDGEMENTS

Thanks to all my friends and family, in particular my brother Michael Gavin, without whom this project would not have been possible. Also thanks to my parents Mick and Anna Gavin, Patrick Gavin, the Henry family, Brian Ó Hairt, Brian Miller, Devin Shepherd, Marta Cook, Kelsey Lutz, Cary Novotny, John Blake, Sean Keegan, The Center for Irish Music, The Eoin McKiernan Library, Rob Gandara and Carbony woodwinds, and to all of the teachers and musicians who have generously shared their music over the years.

ABOUT THE AUTHOR

Uilleann piper and flute player, Seán Gavin, is one of the most highly regarded Irish musicians of his generation. In 2016 he became the first and only musician born outside Ireland to win the prestigious Seán Ó Riada gold medal, and his most recent recording, a collaboration with fiddler Jesse Smith, accompanist John Blake, and bodhran player Johnny "Ringo" McDonagh, was hailed by The Irish Echo as "traditional music at its best!" Seán also tours regularly with the groups Bua and Téada, both of which have gleaned top praise from Irish music critics around the globe. Originally from Detroit, he was encouraged in music by his father Mick, a fiddler from Co. Clare, and his brother Michael - a multi-instrumentalist. At age 12, he started work on the uilleann pipes with the late Al Purcell, former pupil of piper Leo Rowsome. Seán moved to Chicago at age 20 where he spent a decade playing and studying with the Windy City's finest musicians, particularly Sligo flute-legend Kevin Henry (RIP). Seán then spent three years in the twin cities of Minnesota, where he was active in the non-profit Center for Irish Music. Now back in the Detroit area, Seán teaches locally as well as online, and continues to tour both domestically and abroad. Questions or comments? Contact Seán at SeanGavinMusic@gmail.com.

Learn to Play Today
with folk music instruction from Hal Leonard

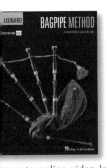

Hal Leonard Bagpipe Method

The Hal Leonard Bagpipe Method is designed for anyone just learning to play the Great Highland bagpipes. This comprehensive and easy-to-use beginner's guide serves as an introduction to the bagpipe chanter. It includes [ac]cess to online video lessons with demonstrations [of] all the examples in the book! Lessons include: the [pr]actice chanter, the Great Highland Bagpipe scale, [ba]gpipe notation, proper technique, grace-noting, [em]bellishments, playing and practice tips, traditional [tu]nes, buying a bagpipe, and much more!
[0]0102521 Book/Online Video $14.99

Hal Leonard Banjo Method – Second Edition

Authored by Mac Robertson, Robbie Clement & Will Schmid. This innovative method teaches 5-string, bluegrass style. The method consists of two instruction books and two cross-referenced [su]pplement books that offer the beginner a care[fu]lly-paced and interest-keeping approach to the [bl]uegrass style.
[0]0699500 Book 1 Only...$9.99
[0]0695101 Book 1 with Online Audio...............$17.99
[0]0699502 Book 2 Only...$9.99
[0]0696056 Book 2 with CD................................$17.99

Hal Leonard Brazilian Guitar Method

by Carlos Arana

This book uses popular Brazilian songs to teach you the basics of the Brazilian guitar style and technique. Learn to play in the styles of Joao Gilberto, Luiz Bonfá, [B]aden Powell, Dino Sete Cordas, Joao Basco, and [m]any others! Includes 33 demonstration tracks.
[0]0697415 Book/Online Audio $17.99

Hal Leonard Chinese Pipa Method

by Gao Hong

This easy-to-use book serves as an introduction to the Chinese pipa and its techniques. Lessons include: tuning • Western & Chinese notation basics • left and right hand techniques • positions • trem[o]lo • bending • vibrato and overtones • classical pipa [r]epertoire • popular Chinese folk tunes • and more!
[0]0121398 Book/Online Video $19.99

Hal Leonard Dulcimer Method – Second Edition

by Neal Hellman

A beginning method for the Appalachian dulcimer with a unique new approach to solo melody and chord playing. Includes tuning, modes and many beautiful folk songs all demonstrated on the audio accompaniment. Music and tablature.
00699289 Book...$12.99
00697230 Book/Online Audio.........................$19.99

Hal Leonard Flamenco Guitar Method

by Hugh Burns

Traditional Spanish flamenco song forms and classical pieces are used to teach you the basics of the style and technique in this book. Lessons cover: strumming, picking and percussive techniques • arpeggios • improvisation • fingernail tips • capos • and much more. Includes flamenco history and a glossary.
00697363 Book/Online Audio $17.99

Hal Leonard Irish Bouzouki Method

by Roger Landes

This comprehensive method focuses on teaching the basics of the instrument as well as accompaniment techniques for a variety of Irish song forms. It covers: playing position • tuning • picking & strumming patterns • learning the fretboard • accompaniment styles • double jigs, slip jigs & reels • drones • counterpoint • arpeggios • playing with a capo • traditional Irish songs • and more.
00696348 Book/Online Audio $12.99

Hal Leonard Mandolin Method – Second Edition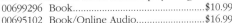

Noted mandolinist and teacher Rich Del Grosso has authored this excellent mandolin method that features great playable tunes in several styles (bluegrass, country, folk, blues) in standard music notation and tablature. The audio features play-along duets.
00699296 Book...$10.99
00695102 Book/Online Audio.........................$16.99

Hal Leonard Oud Method

by John Bilezikjian

This book teaches the fundamentals of standard Western music notation in the context of oud playing. It also covers: types of ouds, tuning the oud, playing position, how to string the oud, scales, chords, arpeggios, tremolo technique, studies and exercises, songs and rhythms from Armenia and the Middle East, and 25 audio tracks for demonstration and play along.
00695836 Book/Online Audio $14.99

Hal Leonard Sitar Method

by Josh Feinberg

This beginner's guide serves as an introduction to sitar and its technique, as well as the practice, theory, and history of raga music. Lessons include: tuning • postures • right- and left-hand technique • Indian notation • raga forms; melodic patterns • bending strings • hammer-ons, pull-offs, and slides • changing strings • and more!
00696613 Book/Online Audio $16.99
00198245 Book/Online Media.........................$19.99

Hal Leonard Ukulele Method

by Lil' Rev

This comprehensive and easy-to-use beginner's guide by acclaimed performer and uke master Lil' Rev includes many fun songs of different styles to learn and play. Includes: types of ukuleles, tuning, music reading, melody playing, chords, strumming, scales, tremolo, music notation and tablature, a variety of music styles, ukulele history and much more.
00695847 Book 1 Only.....................................$7.99
00695832 Book 1 with Online Audio..............$12.99
00695948 Book 2 Only.....................................$7.99
00695949 Book 2 with Online Audio..............$11.99

HAL•LEONARD®

Visit Hal Leonard Online at
www.halleonard.com

Prices and availability subject to change
without notice.